# Ever So Gently

# *Ever So Gently*

## A Collection of Poems

**Lauren Scott**

baydreamerwrites.com

# Contents

# Contents



2

**The Noise, The Laughter, The Chaos, The Loved Ones**

# Contents

3

**Lost in Thought**



{ x }

# Contents

# A Note from the Editor

It was a pleasure for me to edit *Ever So Gently* with Lauren Scott. She and I spent hours meeting monthly in a small coffee shop reading and re-reading her poems.

I am impressed with Lauren's dedication to writing and find her honest, soul-searching look at life to be touching and very well worth reading.

I suggest you curl up with your favorite warm beverage and enjoy this special book.

~ Sharon Bluhm

# *Introduction*

Ever So Gently expresses the gentle demeanor in which I welcome nature's offerings. The gentle way in which I should react to life's challenges. The gentle grace in my heart that is full of gratitude for the love in my life. For the support of family and friends through every stumble and celebration. When I witness another sunrise, I am reminded to breathe and live gently. But succeeding in 'gentle' may not happen around the clock, so if I slip up, I will try again.

Everywhere I turn, a poem is there for the writing. It's in my marriage with my husband, Matt, who is my best friend. From that first delicious kiss to a deeper love that matures over three decades. It's in the memories of when our children became a new bloom in our family garden, or now in a simple conversation with them as adults. Poetry comforts as we experience unexpected health scares or financial setbacks. All of life's experiences provide inspiration for yet another poem. And pondering the rewards and mysteries of life itself inspire me to jot down my ideas before they're lost on the breeze.

Most poems in this collection are free verse. But you'll find a small gathering of syllabic poetry: Haiku, Tanka, Etheree, Shadorma, Didactic Cinquain, Double Ennead, and Oddquain. Style notwithstanding, I hope you'll discover a few poems that evoke a special memory or act as a reminder that you are not alone in living with your emotions. Maybe you'll get a good laugh or experience an 'aha' moment. Above all, when you turn the last page, may you discover the reward of living ever so gently.

# 1

# *The Wisdom of Nature*

# The First Morning

<br>

*Our eyes open to chirps*
*from high in the fir trees,*
*and we hear the rustle*
*of a skittering squirrel.*
*The evening before,*
*every creature became silent*
*as darkness sank into the evening.*
*But this morning,*
*with sunlight*
*caressing the lake,*
*we walk the few steps*
*to calm water,*
*nestle into our chairs*
*and slowly sip our coffee.*
*We listen. Peace.*
*Cottony clouds drift by.*
*We want to move into*
*them, feel their softness*
*enfold us.*
*They shift with the grace*
*of a swan.*
*Ripples shimmer above sand.*
*Art in clear water.*
*And this is when we watch morning happen...*

# Chilling Embrace

*I have been embraced*
*by the chilling presence*
*of loneliness.*
*I have wondered where the niche*
*designed for me exists in this world*
*in which my breaths originate.*
*I have waited for the glow*
*to emerge from behind the shadows.*
*But when I take that soft step*
*into the splendor of nature,*
*listen to the trees whisper their sagacity,*
*feel the flowing rivers move my pain,*
*creating vast distance between it and me,*
*I have been revived by the compassion*
*that nature offers so unselfishly.*

# A Fine Discovery

*Morning light sweeps*
*over the horizon*
*full of adventure,*
*we breathe in fresh air,*
*lungs sigh with pleasure.*

*Slipping arms through straps,*
*his life passion,*
*my curiosity rose at fifty-six*
*one boot in front of the other.*
*Fir and pine trees flank the trail,*
*butterflies the color of snow, so pure,*
*elegantly float from bloom to bloom,*

*the golden sun follows,*
*our thirst sated from water bottles,*
*a slight breeze promises relief*
*like an invigorating dip in fresh water.*

*Resting on the shore, legs stretched,*
*ankles crossed, feeling inconsequential*
*in its vast presence, the surface shines*
*like an exceptional jewel unearthed.*

## *Ever So Gently*

*Relatives by nature,*
*dragonflies, like miniature jets,*
*and damselflies with their blue,*
*iridescent wings, gracefully flit about.*
*Surely, they are aware of our fascination.*

*Tiny threads of peace*
*weave into the marrow of our souls*
*mending any fretting that stirred.*

*A great fortune to play a part with nature*
*in this magical moment of existence,*
*to discover such a gem,*
*just the two of us relishing adventure in our sixties,*
*just the two of us and our loyal backpacks.*

# The Sun Knows

*Evening advances.*
*The shore wears nothing*
*but a few rocks*
*scattered on its sand.*
*In their quiet space,*
*a father and son hold fishing lines*
*hoping their luck will lift.*
*A lone sailboat glides by*
*pausing for the unfolding.*
*With hair the color of an egret,*
*an older man leans against a stump.*

*Clouds understand why we wait.*
*A fine yellow highlighter has*
*delicately outlined their smooth edges.*
*Occasionally, trout jump out of the*
*still water, only a few ripples*
*show their excitement.*

*Then suddenly the sky explodes*
*in tangerines, salmons, canary yellows –*
*brighter with every second.*
*It's as though a painter swished*
*her brush back and forth*
*on the immense backdrop,*

*to the left, to the right,*
*repeating with the grace*
*of an orchestra leader.*
*Can the sun slipping behind*
*downy clouds*
*be more spectacular?*

# In Good Company

*When we stroll among redwood trees,*
*our steps slow down, we are in good company.*
*There is no reason to rush and we won't hesitate*
*to hug them with open arms, because, why not?*
*They deserve reverence for their generosity.*
*In their company, fine fibers of peace*
*flow through our hearts and souls,*
*centering us. Any worries burdening our minds*
*fall to the earth to be walked upon and buried.*
*We listen as their leaves whisper in the breeze,*
*Be filled with joy and do not fret,*
*for there is no time for that nonsense.*

# Boots

*From the trail's draw,*
*we step*
*deeper*
*into*
*solitude,*
*embraced by*
*the strength*
*of the tall bays.*

*Only an*
*occasional crackle*
*breaks the silence.*

# I Wonder

*I wonder if pine needles*
*wiggle in delight*
*until they float to the earth*
*when summer bids farewell*
*and emerald leaves in autumn*
*transform into reds and golds,*

*and I can't help but question*
*if tall pines in which they*
*hang onto for support*
*long to sway in joyful measure.*

*I know I would cheerfully*
*slip on my dancing shoes*
*if the sky above me suddenly*
*exploded in vivid oranges*

*as though hope itself pushed*
*through all the debris*
*that I've allowed to clutter*
*my mind.*

# Front Row Seats

*We know they're trespassing,*
*but it's such a delight*
*to watch them construct*
*their little home.*
*They flit and flutter*
*with small breathers*
*perching on a nearby branch.*
*He looks dashing*
*in his red bowtie,*
*she glows in motherhood.*
*We're excited to welcome*
*a new family*
*to the neighborhood.*
*A lovely show,*
*and how lucky for us*
*to have front row seats.*

# Toots and Circles

*Perhaps he was a Western Screech Owl*
*that I heard outside our bedroom window*
*in the early darkness before the sun*
*fashioned its glorious arrival.*
*I cannot say with conviction,*
*but it is certain he proclaimed his presence*
*with his high-pitched toots.*

*But what I really want to know...*

*was he aware that just before*
*he sang his series of notes*
*our alarm would,*
*in a matter of minutes,*
*sound off in its circle's ringtone?*

*And did he realize at this time*
*when most homes on the street*
*have not awakened,*
*we brew our dark roast*
*then sit together in harmony*
*for soft conversation?*

*That this routine, though simple*
*to some, would not be the same,*

*would not provide the comforting*
*experience if one of us was not present?*

*I shudder to imagine such a scenario...*

*because this early morning moment*
*commenced with the greeting*
*of our neighboring friend in nature*

*is happening now,*
*and now with my love is where I desire to be.*


(Previously published on Spillwords Press)

# Our Patio Guest

*I don't always watch the news.*
*Doom and gloom seem to*
*monopolize the channels,*
*and my heart hangs heavy*
*before a day has even begun.*

*I want to leap into the sun,*
*feel its warmth and joy,*
*and when it's time to dance*
*in the rain, the cleansing of*
*her gentle drops will*
*refresh me all over again.*

*So, my husband is my channel.*
*He'll convey anything critical,*
*such as,*
*the world will end tomorrow.*

*How is one to move forward*
*carrying such sorrow*
*in their hearts?*

*Then in late afternoon,*
*the patio beckons,*
*the warm breeze*

pirouettes around our faces,
and we are not surprised
to see our familiar guest,
wings thrumming,
soaring to the bright pink petals
in the vast blue.

It is in this moment,
enlightening to my
heart and soul,
I am reminded
of the wonders of life.

# The Hummingbird's Quest

*We hold our breath.*
*Its wings flutter at a possible*
*eighty times per second, so we've read.*

*It closes the distance between us,*
*and we know it eyes the dangling*
*rosy petals. But below those blossoms*
*lies the sleeping dog. He wouldn't be*
*the least bit interested in the winged*
*creature, but the winged creature*
*doesn't know this to be true.*

*And so, we watch our tiny friend*
*flit to within a few feet of the blooms,*
*then disappointment lands in our thoughts*
*as it retreats to the maple,*
*camouflaged to the naked eye.*

*If only it could be brave.*
*If only it knew there was no threat below*
*from the eighty-pound sleeping beast.*
*In fact, the beast quietly snores,*
*and we are confident*
*he is dreaming of squirrels.*

# Wilted Spirits

*Fresh raindrops*
*gently landed*
*on their wilted spirits*
*as I witnessed them lifting*
*with a sigh of relief.*
*Oh, how grateful I feel*
*to absorb the rhythm*
*of the pitter-patter.*

# Sunflower Satisfaction

*With a sense of wonder*
*and newfound delight,*
*I watch them sprout -*
*entering into the land*
*of blossoms and buzzing,*
*a gift unto all*
*beneath the golden light.*

# I Want to Tell Them

*I want to tell them,*
*"Stay among the tall oaks*
*where birds perch on branches*
*feather to feather,*
*and squirrels skitter about...*

*you'll be safe and unseen,*
*except for your antlers*
*and long, spindly legs.*
*Let your keen sense*
*of hearing guide you."*

*But how can I, when in the heat*
*of summer, the sun's rays blaze,*
*and water hasn't caressed the hills?*
*The earth, parched like Chile's Atacama.*

*When, in fact, they can trot*
*a short distance onto our street*
*where dampness rests inside petals*
*of hundreds of blooms.*

*Should I deny them this life-saving sweetness?*
*If not, then how can I teach them to be street smart?*

# October's Miracle

*I forgot how the sound of rain could be soothing
like the calming rhythm of classical music.*

*The thirst for relief had felt longer than eternity,
for the soil exhaled and my lantana sang "Hallelujah!"*

*Silk-thread drizzles dusted rooftops and parched hills
with the flowing grace of an unhurried waterfall.*

*The fascination of puddles slipped my mind,
the childlike sense of play from a hop and a splash.*

*And who would think the sight of cocoa-brown mud
could be so entertaining in all its messiness!*

*Would you believe if I said the flowers smiled at me?
And their leaves offered a gentle wave?*

*Observing from my slightly opened window,
I caught a grateful sigh from the soaked earth,
and I enjoyed listening to the roots laugh in delight.*

# The Peach Rose

*feeling quite bashful*
*she shares her stunning profile*
*nature's loveliness*

*dazzling passersby*
*her peach essence entrances*
*they pause to admire*

*energy restored*
*she reclaims her place in life*
*after night's spring rain*

*raindrops vacillate*
*layers hold their own secrets*
*delicate delight*

*petals of velvet*
*invite raindrops to bask in*
*their peach enchantment*

# Bougainvillea

*her vibrant petals*
*thrive, loaded with attitude,*
*mysteries disguised*

# Summer Brilliance

*summer's palette gleams*
*a glorious apparel*
*she loves to showcase*

# Feathered Friends

*seed bell entices*
*finches fly in for landing*
*scrub jay constructs plans*

*no need to squabble*
*abundance of sustenance*
*nibble in delight*

*escaping the noise*
*watching nature's performance*
*silence for the soul*

# Lantana

*I stroll through the yard*
*a dehydrated garden*
*drought drains energy*
*but it perseveres, soaking*
*up occasional showers.*

*Follow its guidance,*
*no surrendering, only*
*joy imparts with ease.*
*Even through difficulties,*
*cause to celebrate appears.*

# Seasonal Blanket

*autumn's dawn blushes*
*in warm hues of coziness*
*melodious crunch*

# Firestorm

*warm colors*
*of new season turn*
*into bold*
*red-hot flames*
*producing tremendous loss*
*beyond heartrending -*
*where once were*
*houses lie keepsakes,*
*sifting through*
*toxic ash*
*moving forward now, nothing*
*but anxiety*

# Territory

*Traveling*
*they wander with grace*
*tall lean legs*
*ears alert*
*eyes look in all directions*
*first-time buyers in*
*the quiet*
*neighborhood, humans*
*intruded,*
*hurried cars,*
*they meet their senseless demise*
*one more point for man*

# Messages from the Sea

*listen intently*
*inhale, exhale, feel the calm*
*your soul will thank you*

*secrets ride the waves*
*ebbing, flowing in turquoise*
*we are not privy*

*whispers in the surf*
*ambiguous to discern*
*relish in their song*

# Tiny Treasures

*rocks and shiny shells*
*in all shapes and colors make*
*young hearts sing and dance*

*precious works of art*
*remain forever priceless*
*time irrelevant*

*sandy shore offers*
*troves of tiny treasures for*
*imaginations*

*fingers hold paintbrush*
*brows furrow, fully focused*
*masterpiece crafted*

# Three Men in a Boat

*Lake*
*early morn*
*cold air touches warm*
*water, steam rises, halo*
*~ calm ~*

*They*
*hear whispers*
*the lake is calling*
*geese witness from shore, unseen*
*~ truth ~*

*Luck,*
*will it change?*
*floating on glass-like*
*surface, poles dangle with lures*
*~ bite ~*

*ball*
*of golden*
*tones ascends, bringing*
*possibilities with its*
*~ glow ~*

# Poppies, Rainwater, Summertime

**Poppies**
*Bright, cheerful*
*Swaying, smiling, waving*
*As I drive by*
*Blooms*

**Rainwater**
*Cool, necessary*
*Refreshing, quenching, soothing*
*Brings life to nature*
*Precipitation*

**Summertime**
*Warm, colorful*
*Swimming, relaxing, vacationing*
*Get outdoors and play*
*Solstice*

# Blushing Bonsai

*I am short in height*
*a little thick in middle*
*stress-free maintenance*

*stodgy short stature*
*decked out in handsome fashion*
*sturdy in nature*

*I'm adorable*
*according to my owner*
*my leaves are blushing*

# 2

# The Noise, The Laughter, The Chaos, The Loved Ones

# The World is Broken

*The world is broken,*
    *we are aware,*
        *but being alive on this crisp autumn morning,*

*what a blessing*
        *to behold*

*And he says,*
*"The good news*
*for today is*
*I love you,*
*Your heart,*
*Your mind,*
*Your soul."*

*The world may be broken,*
        *but I am not.*

(Previously published on Spillwords Press)

# I Didn't Know Him Then

*I didn't know him then on that high school campus.*
*I didn't pass him by in the halls of science.*

*He blended into any group wherever his feet landed.*
*In language of his peers, his name was branded.*

*I played the wallflower having one special niche.*
*Music, my haven, just across the bridge.*

*Popularity didn't find me. He sported a football jersey.*
*My legs marched in drill team. The players didn't see me.*

*He gave his whole heart for it to be returned.*
*I also gave mine for it to be scorned.*

*Then in between the lines, life metamorphosed into better.*
*The reason happened for us, our paths meandered together.*

# In Technicolor

*A distant memory*
*in technicolor...*
*I want to rip the page*
*from my mind's photo album*
*because my heart was foolish*
*to fall for that man,*
*our skies different*
*our dreams astray,*
*but the heart's pulse*
*beats to a tune*
*of its own choosing,*
*logic holds no leverage.*
*Though this man*
*wasn't a cockroach,*
*I never wished*
*to stomp on him.*
*So I am grateful,*
*for without that page*
*I wouldn't have*
*stumbled*
*upon the path*
*that lead me*
*to my love at last.*

# If the Universe Would Share

*I whisper to him,*
*"Do you see that blue*
*luminous star?*
*I choose it for you."*
*If the universe would share,*
*I'd pull the gleaming beauty*
*from the constellations*
*and place it in the palm*
*of his hands.*
*We would sit upon*
*a slow-moving cloud*
*and dangle our legs*
*into freedom.*
*I'd tenderly touch*
*my lips to his,*
*hunger reeling*
*through our veins,*
*tumbling us into a*
*pleasant intoxication,*
*watching moonbeams*
*pierce our private night sky.*

# Tender Reminiscence

*I recall our younger years*
*how he'd touch his lips to mine*
*while standing on the step*
*when we cold-shouldered time.*
*No desire of letting go*
*new love holding us near.*
*No care in the world*
*in the moment that we shared.*
*Who knew those doorstep kisses*
*would carry us this distance?*
*(floating in a state-of-mind*
*of tender reminiscence)*

# Healdsburg

*Over three decades to celebrate, we drive north up the coast*
*passing lush green hills of January, gripping wheel from wind's thrust.*

*The plaza pulls us in with its charm, windows entice with appealing apparel,*
*sun blazes, temperature warm, shops shimmer in their zeal for patrons.*

*"You look like I need a drink of wine," words on a hand towel with pizzazz.*
*"With every glass of wine comes wisdom," a neighboring towel adds.*

*Shelves stocked with crafts, cheery, persuading to purchase without effort.*
*Feeling like we're in Rose Apothecary, where are David and Patrick?*

*Arches and patios display lights for when the moon shines her splendor.*
*We feast on pulled pork and slaw, Chardonnay and Pliney the Elder.*

*Picnics on blankets, a man strums and sings like Paul Simon.*
*A man with a backpack eyes the banquets, a dog licks his chops with a plan.*

*Great eats and drinks, and fun souvenirs, cash spent, plastic card dented,*
*toasting to these decades, moments to share, two hearts blended.*

# First Breath

*With every new miracle of life*
*answers aren't scripted in the stars,*
*but I knew since your very first breath*
*my life would become yours.*

*Through innocent eyes and curious touch*
*each new discovery you shared,*
*your smile grew bigger than the sun,*
*your heart's elation declared.*

*You stowed dreams in the clouds,*
*imaginings rose higher than the heavens.*
*Cuddling you in that first euphoric light*
*made me fall in love with you in seconds.*

*Life has blossomed into delight and wonder*
*in every part of its glowing greatness,*
*and with each ounce of my being,*
*my enduring love for you is ageless.*

# Beneath the Big, Golden Sun

*He was their hero when they were young,*
*teaching of nature beneath the big golden sun.*
*They tried on their packs before feet hit the trail.*
*He'd say, "Be prepared or else you could fail."*

*The trio trekked down paths and up inclines too,*
*pausing along the way to admire a flower or two.*
*After arriving in camp, they helped pitch the tent,*
*stakes in the ground, windows unzipped to vent.*

*As an Arborist, he educated them about trees*
*under the blue sky beside the buzzing honeybees.*
*They explored the ground seeking burrowing bugs.*
*He expressed praise with words and loving hugs.*

*When the sun faded at the end of a day,*
*they roasted marshmallows, found dominoes to play.*
*His first goal was fun in nature, then came self-reliance.*
*Their minds were like sponges, soaking up the science.*

*Now they reminisce for the best teacher he was*
*and recall the bonding with the deepest of love.*
*Now he's proud of them, adulting and doing it well,*
*honored with the memories, the special stories to tell.*

# Young Campers

*They amble through the African savannah,*
*eyes alert, keeping watch for big animals*
*seeking out their next meal.*
*But their excitement also escalates*
*because they want to see the*
*beautiful creatures.*
*Suddenly, a thunder-booming growl*
*echoes throughout the grassland!*
*Their feet become blocks of cement,*
*stopping in their tracks,*
*as fear creeps up their necks!*
*Terror escalates as they hold their breath!*
*Legs shake like trees from an*
*angry gust of wind!*
*Any sound could be the end!*

*Then Mom yells, "Lunch is ready!"*
*Fear subsides, and their adventure halts.*

*Until tomorrow ...*
*when their imaginations come alive again.*

# A Little Bit More

*She'd sit on the landing, long hair cascading,*
*her little friends listening to her reading about Paddy,*
*Peter the Rabbit, and The Three Little Bears.*

*She'd stand in the middle of her room, fingers wrapped*
*around her hairbrush-microphone, singing her heart out…*
*Nashville in her dreams.*

*Now, a beautiful woman giving life her best*
*with an open heart, a sunflower smile.*

*Her world has expanded without me…*

*Geography intervenes, and yet, we have phone chats!*
*Hours later, what could we have gabbed about?*

*Everything, and most likely, a little bit more.*

*I'm sure she knows the amount of residence*
*she claims in my heart. Then again, it is quite*
*difficult to quantify.*

*It would be like counting the display of gleaming stars*
*in the vast evening sky.*

# The Mess

*I find comfort in the clothes*
*strewn on the floor*
*soon to be dumped in the washer,*
*wallet lying on the dresser,*
*cell charging, bed comforter*
*in shambles*

*because the messiness*
*displays his presence.*

*Now with air miles accumulated*
*back in his time zone,*
*the room shines in all its cleanliness,*
*the neatness grating on my nerves,*
*the silence, a cold shoulder.*

*My hand pulls back the comforter,*
*tousling, creating wrinkles*
*in the navy fabric, then I pull*
*some old shirts from the closet,*
*tossing them on the floor.*

*I can certainly pretend*
*he's just out with friends...*

# The Same Sky

*I don't know if I should feel embarrassed*
*about having a moment that lasted for a day,*
*and there is no point in fighting the tears.*
*They are winners.*

*Would other parents think differently?*
*Not that I care because...*

*I loathe the many miles between us*
*as though they have done me*
*wrong, becoming my enemy.*

*But the consolation is knowing*
*when my eyes look upward,*
*when I exhale acceptance,*
*we share the same vivid blue sky.*

*The distance, simply geography.*

# The Travelers


*In early years when promises lined up*
*on their doorstep, they were excited*
*to roam streets of Italy, savor pasta,*
*sip Frappato,*
*stroll through France in a cloud of romance,*
*drive roads of Ireland flanked by lush green*
*countryside.*
*But as time whirled by, they learned*
*plans can be navigated only so far.*
*They haven't sipped Frappato*
*or witnessed that countryside...yet.*
*Still, over mountains, through down pours*
*and gusty winds, and days when*
*sherbet-colored skies lifted their spirits,*
*their fingers stayed entwined.*
*Not only has love in their hearts prevailed,*
*but cravings still carbonate for each other.*
*It seems they have traveled*
*the trip of a lifetime.*

# Lucky Girl

*She was never really that social.*
*In fact, if she didn't look like a dog,*
*I would say she was more of a feline.*
*You know, the independent type.*
*Not unfriendly, but quite content*
*in her own company.*

*She'd sniff around the bushes*
*and the trees on her walks,*
*relishing each new scent...*

*In the house, she'd follow the sun*
*before plopping down and curling*
*up for a nap.*

*Occasionally, we'd find her*
*cozied up in her corner of the sofa,*
*legs folded, body curved, forming*
*a perfect circle.*

*Where is she now, I wonder...*
*not visible in this physical world.*
*And yet, we feel her with us.*
*She answered to "Lucky"*
*but we were the lucky ones.*

# The Blue Down Jacket

*The radio belted out "Joy to the World!"*
*You were a teenage boy, but on this*
*Christmas morning in '75, excitement*
*buzzed! Your dad watched and listened,*
*relaxed in his corner chair, but your mom*
*played Santa, just as jolly! The first time*
*we met. Do you remember?*

*You and your dad hiked Half Dome that year,*
*then...the many trips we booked...*
*those rocky inclines had my sleeves shaking!*
*Hiking to Italy Pass, 12,000 feet at the top!*
*We did it! Trekking through the Trinity Alps,*
*Thousand Island Lake in the Sierra.*
*And Mount Shasta!*
*I kept you warm when the air was ice.*

*What a team we made, and I couldn't believe*
*how beautiful the world could be...*

*Then with the years your adolescence faded like*
*my blue dye, but I stayed loyal. Why wouldn't I?*
*You are my brother, even still, all grown up*
*with a family of your own.*

### *Ever So Gently*

*Lucky is what I feel because ages ago, I thought*
*I'd be buried beneath piles of clothes at the bottom*
*of a bag to be given away.*
*But mostly, I feel privileged for my significance.*
*I recall her vividly.*
*She left this world too young, too soon.*

*You see, when we hang out,*
*your memories transport you*
*to that morning when her laughter was music,*
*her smile was sunlight,*
*her energy as vibrant as "Joy to the World."*
*You travel to the special place in your mind*
*when your mom was still in your life.*

# Copper Boy

*He carries eighty pounds of love*
*when he trots around on his long legs,*
*and those amber eyes see right into our souls.*

*His white choppers shine as if*
*they've never caused any commotion...*
*never mind when he attempted*
*to eat the barbecue!*

*When he hears a knock on the door,*
*his bark echoes across the Golden Gate,*
*along the marina into San Francisco.*
*Out of protection? Sure. But mostly from excitement.*

*A social butterfly sporting a Labrador costume,*
*that's what he is... freely passing out his affection,*
*assuming everyone loves his slobbery kisses.*

*But he has a selfish side, rolling over on his back,*
*expecting a belly rub, and his ears feel like silk*
*between our fingers. How can we deny his wishes?*
*We can't get enough...*

*He loves unconditionally. He never wastes*
*one precious minute worrying about world events*

*or whether the pandemic is here to stay.*
*And he is never one to judge.*

*He just loves in his simple way, and we love him back.*
*And that is simply enough.*

# Castanets

Stepping outside, I stroll down<br>
the quiet road with my lab on my left,<br>
his gait graceful as a galloping horse<br>
in slow motion.<br>
Squirrels raise their sleepy heads<br>
in this early hour.<br>
The sky coal black, but around the corner,<br>
watermelon pinks, corals, and lemon yellows<br>
take center stage.<br>
My camera doesn't do justice.<br>
Then my son's wisdom echoes<br>
in my mind, "Enjoy the moment."<br>
I slip that device in my pocket.<br>
To my right, salmon-colored roses<br>
flaunt their fragrance – I am intoxicated.<br>
Passing orange poppies, their stems<br>
flutter with excitement, eager for<br>
the sun's ascent, and in the distance,<br>
silence sings its serene ballad.<br>
As the tempo of our pace speeds up,<br>
a breeze joins us,<br>
and the leaves on the trees<br>
lining the lane sway in rhythm<br>
as though dancing a waltz.<br>
Jowls flap, he smiles with brown nose

*set in overdrive. The sun's gentle touch*
*adds a glimmer to his copper coat.*
*I pause, bending down to his level,*
*fingers stroke shiny, silky fur,*
*his eyes close, contented from contact.*

*When we move again, his nails on asphalt*
*mimic the clicking of two sets of castanets,*
*and in seconds, I realize these observations*
*are what life is all about...*
*seeing...feeling...smelling...listening...being.*

# Little Cabin

*Oh, little cabin,*
*what joy you brought*
*within your barn red shutters*
*on your large corner lot.*

*Oh, little cabin,*
*the laughter you embraced*
*within your walls of wood,*
*the love interlaced.*

*Lasagna, a staple,*
*Spices in the air,*
*meals at the white table*
*with black and silver dinnerware.*

*Memories for a family of five*
*among tall sugar pines.*
*Oh, little cabin on the mountain,*
*Oh, little cabin divine.*

# The Tiny Town

*As the baby of three daughters, a decade younger in age,*
*my narrative reads differently along with setting and stage.*
*I was only ten years old, but Dad's job was important.*
*I didn't want to leave friends, but I moved without argument.*
*The tiny town didn't own a dot on the map,*
*a K-mart for excitement and land that lay flat.*
*No trees flanked roads with leaves falling like snowflakes,*
*but the sky was just as blue as the sky in my home state.*

*Old friends and I stayed connected minus cell phones.*
*New friendships were to be formed in the unfamiliar time zone.*
*Layer and layer of red brick, the construct of our three-bedroom,*
*snowfall enchanted in chill of winter but melted from rays too soon.*
*Four years zoomed by before boxes were packed again,*
*heading back to where we came from to be nearer to kin.*
*Another set of friends to miss, tough when moving so young,*
*transferring schools midyear, another beginning undone.*

*Children wish parents were perfect, but they carry their own flaws.*
*When I reminisce to these years, memories make me pause...*
*to a time when I witnessed their laughter and tears,*
*how their love embraced me in those formative years.*
*Memories shift to the porch stretching east to west,*
*white pillars stood tall, a chapter I gave my best.*

# Blanket of Gold

*I look across the backyard with a heavy sigh,*
*just a few weeks ago, the broom had done its*
*job, the garden gloves lie in the shed, caked*
*with flakes of dirt, exhausted from pulling*
*weeds that had the nerve to sprout abundantly,*
*as though they are admired as much as*
*the glorious lavender hydrangeas.*

*Now, crunchy yellow leaves cover the grass,*
*as if Mother Nature gently laid down*
*a blanket of gold. The wardrobe changes*
*of the leaves, pirouetting to the ground,*
*lead to the season when Gratitude is placed*
*on a pedestal, paying homage even more*
*than on any given day,*
*which leads us to the turkey brining*
*in a citrusy concoction. The carving knife*
*and gravy ladle eager to present their annual*
*performance. The formal dinnerware excited*
*to display its shiny patina. The gathering.*

*And on this special day, the sky and sun*
*will collaborate to create a bright blue backdrop,*
*no clouds invited to this celebration,*
*not even a breath of wind will drift through,*

or one tiny raindrop will fall on this event,
just a temperature cool enough
to welcome a sweater,
the kind of weather that delights.

Before sitting down, he would ask for a beverage,
and then even after sinking into the soft sofa,
his hand would caress the glass for minutes.
He would pause before taking a sip.

Before joining in the festivities,
he, who lived through the second world war,
would slowly absorb
the noise,
the laughter,
the chaos,
the loved ones...

# Gumdrops

*They stepped inside Grandma's house...*
*their eyes zeroed in*
*on the white candy dish,*
*painted in pink and*
*pale green flowers.*
*They looked at her with imploring eyes,*
*she nodded in approval.*
*Their young hands*
*lifted the lid*
*where inside the dish*
*they found magic!*
*Gumdrops in colors*
*of the rainbow!*
*With each bite into cherry,*
*grape, orange, and lemon,*
*their smiles grew bigger.*
*She relished in their happiness*
*that felt like a warm blanket*
*wrapped around her aging body,*
*and as much as she loved buying*
*those gumdrops that painted*
*joy on their cute little faces,*
*the magical candy dish was only*
*one way she showed the love*
*in her heart for them.*

# The Old Afghan

*Each purl stitch was interwoven with love*
*from her gentle touch.*
*She, the teacher, me, the student,*
*as our bodies sank into the sofa*
*checkered in a 70's palette.*

*For a new teen, my love for her was unmeasured.*
*Now, fully immersed in motherhood*
*after three decades, the mom role is clear as glass,*
*how heart and mind require flexibility,*
*the juggling of many hats.*

*Her wisdom often mingles with my thoughts*
*when I whisper, "I get it, Mom."*
*Teardrops of love struggle for freedom,*
*grief clutches at my heart.*

*Autumn browns, reds, yellows, and oranges*
*from that afghan warmed memories over*
*the years, but at some point, my novice knitwork*
*must have slipped a stitch because those warm shades*
*unraveled through the seasons, crafting a hole in the center*
*that mirrors the chasm in my heart from missing her.*

# Mom's Plea

*I remember our conversation...*
*the effort it took*
*to calm my emotions,*
*phone glued to my ear*
*like a natural extension.*
*Days later Mom asked Dad,*
*"When will this be over?"*
*He could be gentle or*
*travel the path of honesty.*
*I don't know the words*
*he pulled from*
*a seventy-year love...*
*how he tenderly tiptoed*
*through the syllables,*
*since his heart*
*was shattering*
*into millions*
*of tiny fragments.*
*Her time was close.*
*Our awareness vigilant.*
*Each day,*
*another breath held*
*until the hands of time*
*would pause.*
*Then as quickly*

*as a gray sky opens
on a winter day,
she had ascended.
Memories of her
loving spirit
followed in the
years to come.
But not one day passes
without her gracing our
thoughts.
Not one day slips by
without her knowing
our lives are changed
forever.*

# She Listens

*He cares for his father whose body tires,*
*pain raging at cyclone force*
*from one hundred years of living a lifetime.*
*Yes, one hundred years! We were thrilled*
*to celebrate this monumental milestone,*
*but our emotions undulate –*
*who wishes to watch a loved one suffer?*

*Another week of work comes to an end.*
*With glass of wine in hand, we exhale*
*on the patio. Then the sun says,*
*"Good night, my dear friends," as he*
*descends, making room for the moon.*

*And when the moon appears, Oh, my!*
*She takes our breath away!*
*Bright and bold as if she senses*
*we could use light in our souls.*
*She pays attention,*
*but most importantly, she listens.*
*And though the stars act a bit bashful,*
*they eavesdrop, and we are fine that they do.*

*The moon and stars hear us,*
*just an ordinary couple enjoying*

a Friday evening but with heavy hearts.
Their absolute attention, imagine this,
out of all eyes gazing at the brilliant sky –
we know the moon's lustrous presence
is for us alone.

Then we rise from our seats and head into
the house, feeling relaxed from the wine's
fluidity, and appreciative that our troubles
have been received.

# Diane

*a caring, soft force*
*a disciplinarian*
*heart teeming with love*
*her circle embraced the warmth*
*from her glimmering essence*

*poppy-orange painted*
*fingernails matched her kind smile*
*her laugh contagious*
*lifting wavering spirits*
*always spreading elation*

*she blessed our marriage*
*twenty-four months was her time,*
*tendered memories*
*nourishing our emotions*
*unbeknown the grief to come*

*time swiftly progressed*
*cancer penetrated her*
*soul, the oxygen*
*tank accompanied us on*
*that cold day in December*

we slid onto faux
leather, an afternoon lunch
the horizon bleak
her love flowed into my heart
strong emotions untethered

fifty-nine was her
final number of candles
on her apple pie
a haunting, morning phone call
altering lives forever

# The Timepiece

*To*
*the teen,*
*Edward was*
*like a grandpa*
*and dear friend to the*
*boy's grandma, Mabel, at*
*a time when she persevered*
*through an unforgettable loss.*
*Sounds of war vibrated ruthlessly.*
*Women were placed in subordinate roles.*
*A pocket watch, timeless in its essence,*
*a present, golden in tone and worth.*
*Locomotive chugs down the tracks,*
*a double turn makes it tick,*
*heartbeat of fifty years.*
*Poignant history,*
*memories to*
*visit now*
*and then,*
*time.*

# Little Sister Memories

*sudden highway trip*
*time escaped crossing state lines*
*solo with cassettes*

*parents not privy*
*sister played supporting role*
*to lessen their fret*

*turquoise entices*
*refreshing in summer fun*
*laps, giggles, splashes*

*pink restaurant dressed*
*in fifties decor, her treat*
*for sister night out*

*pie slices the size*
*of a 33 LP*
*two forks to indulge*

*slumber party at*
*studio near Disneyland*
*rom-com movie night*

*memories never to be forgotten, sisters first, friends forever*

# I was Adopted

Written from the perspective of Copper, The Labrador


*Two dogs lived with me*
*a kind woman cared for us*
*but it wasn't home*
*I waited for the feeling*
*then they walked through the front door*

*girl, boy, and mother*
*spoke to me, gentle voices*
*showing interest*
*mother and woman shook hands*
*I jumped in the car, smiling*

*sniffing in the yard*
*marking my territory*
*sniffing through the house*
*each corner felt like comfort*
*finally, I found my home*

*mom, Dad, and children*
*walked me, played chase, tennis balls*

***Ever So Gently***

*somersaulted on*
*soft grass. Fetching was fun, but*
*letting go I did not like*

*they taught me commands*
*to sit, stay, come, heal, lie down*
*I love to shake paw*
*I learned quickly and got treats*
*and lots of loving cuddles*

*humans say time flies*
*almost thirteen, I'm old now*
*but with my people*
*who don't hit, kick, or starve me*
*I am loved and protected*

*sad faces on screen*
*anger hearts of compassion*
*unthinkable acts*
*please throw them your safety net*
*adoption saves lives for all*

# The Giver

*He pulls me*
*into myself so*
*I may see*
*qualities*
*he loved from the beginning*
*though his perception*
*runs deeper –*
*mine, a trace of clouds,*
*then he lifts*
*my heart and*
*soul to the starlit sky where*
*our dreams become us.*

# Last Conversation with Dad

*Sunday afternoon*
*blue sky stretches forever*
*he hears my words, but*
*his voice offers no response*
*silent for eternity*

*his body, a shell,*
*an emotional Monday*
*lonely life chapter*

# 3

# *Lost in Thought*

# Darker than the Deepest Sea

*Life is like a package wrapped in festive paper.*
*The matching ribbons fascinate in their delicate,*
*entwined company, fingers gently unravel,*
*heartbeats increase from excitement.*
*We lift the lid, peek inside, letting our*
*inner child frolic to the forefront of our minds.*

*But unlike recyclable paper, the gift of life*
*cannot be tossed back into the universe.*
*There is no spare awaiting on the sidelines,*
*and we should be mindful that the contents*
*require tenderness with instructions solely*
*for each one of us individually,*
*because as visible as a ruby rose*
*in a garden of white daisies...*

*we are beautifully unique.*

*Once we follow these*
*with gratitude and vivacity,*
*the purpose of our gift will reveal itself*
*as naturally as moonlight on a night*
*darker than the deepest sea.*

# Maybe

<br>

*When you sit by the window,*
*evading life's demands,*
*watching hummingbirds*
*flit about, do you wonder*
*if our existence is the only*
*breathing form?*
*Who's to assume we're alone*
*with stars millions of miles*
*away glistening in the night?*
*Maybe other beings wonder*
*if they are simply*
*a tiny atom or molecule*
*floating in the larger picture.*
*Maybe we're just a raindrop*
*in someone else's universe.*

# 7 a.m.

The sun slowly opens
its sleepy eyes
The neighborhood
still breathes
soft breaths

Not a soul
Not a sound

We own this moment
This moment is ours

Tranquility flows
through our veins
We exhale gratitude
Another miracle
reveals itself
in the creation
of a new dawn.

# Opening

*This poem isn't meant to imply the end-all.*
*It really shouldn't, nor does it intend*
*to lug around such a label...too much liability.*

*Instead, it dreams of opening like soft petals*
*of a springtime bloom reveling*
*in the first kiss of sunshine.*

*It wishes to open like the door of a cottage*
*adorned in pastel blues and delicate yellows,*
*welcoming you inside*

*as if to offer tea and shortbread*
*so you might feel relaxed,*
*but most of all, so you would feel accepted.*

# Things I Know, Believe, and Imagine

*I know hearts can shatter if beaten down,*
*and souls can be crushed if pounded,*
*and those judging others*
*appear to be close-minded.*
*I believe people should live*
*the life they were intended.*

*I believe differences afford knowledge.*
*Why is violence the solution*
*for those who loathe a culture or religion?*

*I imagine everyone opening their*
*hearts and minds...*
*Can you envision this landscape,*
*like spring blooming every day,*
*budding across borders and state lines?*
*A glorious bridge connecting us all...*
*if only.*

*I know the ideals of respecting*
*and accepting will stay models*
*to be repeated until the narratives*
*mend, and I hope they do,*

because no one deserves to exist
beneath a cloud of pretense.
I believe all people should
have the freedom to live
within the arms of truth.

I can imagine how invisible scars
create hell for the heart.

I believe Love should remain
the center of all humankind,
but since hate continues to linger
on the streets,
here's a question to ponder...
what should we do differently?

# The Sign

*Just look at the color in the sky!*
*Brush strokes of orange,*
*cheerful like California Poppies*
*parading in our yards.*

*Can you feel it?*

*Hope is clearly suspended*
*in the sunrise*
*in the midst of that vibrancy,*
*waiting for the right time*
*to glide in.*

*That's what we do, isn't it?*
*We wait for the best time,*
*to speak words of honesty*
*or vulnerability.*
*We delay in beginning the next goal.*

*Sometimes, waiting is the right thing to do*
*because we know...*

*It's coming...time...*

*But what if while waiting, we miss the sign?*

# Giggles

*I can still elicit memories*
*of when our block teemed*
*with giggles*
*echoing in the distance,*
*the tapping of shoes on asphalt.*
*Remember hide and seek?*
*They'd take cover*
*behind bushes,*
*parked cars, corner fences.*
*But where are they now?*
*Giggles and footsteps*
*are silent, and yet,*
*not one for sale sign*
*sits in a front yard.*
*Perhaps, sneaky screens*
*stole that amusement,*
*those precious moments*
*spent outdoors*
*under the clear sky,*
*even in rain's gentlest*
*sprinkling,*
*but weather, irrelevant,*
*the friendships mattered.*

# Whispers from the Highway

*Whispers enter dreams*
*the endless highway calls*
*the golden ball will rise*
*Eagles "Take it Easy"*
*under the bluest of skies.*

*No one can discern what lies*
*beyond the other side*
*but adventures flow*
*through veins*
*where options open wide.*

*The road whispers its plea*
*utters promises*
*a direction leading to peace*
*worries tossed to the wind*
*seeking sweet release.*

*Time waits for no one*
*don't assume there is more*
*live fully before it's taken -*
*past the long stretch ahead*
*shines a light to awaken.*

# Ever So Gently

*Whispers enter dreams*
*the endless highway calls*
*the golden ball will rise*
*Eagles "Take it Easy"*
*a call to improvise.*

# A Detour

*It doesn't matter the position of sun or moon*
*or where my feet land...*
*whispers find me,*
*their tasks needing my attention*
*at that very moment.*

*Do they wiggle into your mind, too,*
*like an annoying song repeating on a loop?*

*I question if this busyness is urgent enough*
*to prevent us from breathing in*
*the fragrance of flowers or admiring*
*the pageantry of wildlife outside our windows.*

*Surely our minds piled high with clutter,*

*deserve a detour for some sweet refuge*
*now and then.*

# Nonchalance

*Sometimes
kindness finds itself
in the wrong hands,
wrung out
like a sopping
wet towel,*

*tightly, tightly,*

*drip,*

*drip,*

*drip,*

*with such
nonchalance
as if kindness
is so easily obtained.*

# Unexpected

*Breathe,*
*slowly...*

*blood draws,*
*beeping,*
*scans,*

*opened*
*floodgates...*

*I didn't need*
*reminding*
*of tomorrow's*
*fragility.*

*I was aware...*

*my modest corner in the world*
*had been stained gray.*

*Now, I must dig deep*
    *to find the mindset needed*
        *to change the color.*

# Mirrors

*The mirror causes distress, so I let out a sigh.*
*Moments I'd rather not be me, myself, or I.*
*I've missed visits from those warm smiles.*
*Flaws have flickered through the miles.*

*My body, a tale I'd prefer to let alone.*
*I'll refrain from complaints that I voice at home.*

*It's time to relocate that mirror so telling*
*and pause negative thoughts propelling.*
*But I won't move it, not one single inch!*
*My beautiful body doesn't deserve The Grinch!*

*My legs carry me wherever I prompt them.*
*My arms hug my loved ones again and again.*
*My stomach grew larger with babies in tow,*
*My hips gave them plenty of room to grow.*

*So after time with myself and deep consideration,*
*to my body I will show more honest appreciation.*

# One Thing is Certain

*Have you ever sensed*
*the tingling of a feeling*
*arriving without a label?*
*It stirs through your reflections,*
*your layers, and you walk around*
*in a daze where reality offers*
*no place of comfort.*
*So, the sun sets for the moon,*
*but what does this clarify?*
*One thing is certain -*
*within the constellations,*
*among the celestial stars,*
*this emotion finds balance,*
*treasuring the safety*
*it has stumbled upon.*

# Rings

One foot first, then the other, he stepped inside,
warm ambience enfolded him, greetings from
arms open wide...friendly faces, smiles seemingly sincere,

but for only seconds before those friendly arms
turned on him, pushing him out as smiles vanished
into murky atmosphere.

He stumbled backwards over the darkened line
not to be missed.
(it was there for their purpose)
A tug from the 'welcome' being extracted
out of his heart gave him pause.

How many rings? How far from the inner circle did he land?

And does it really matter?

# Friendships Gone

*Their presence graced my universe*
*beautifully like an endless ceiling*
*of bright blue sky. Then they were gone,*
*as though stealing away in the night,*
*their existence nonexistent.*
*Iron-gray clouds engulfed the blue*
*like a quick brush stroke of gloom.*
*I suspected the sun had an attitude,*
*refusing to rise. And each new day*
*magnified the question: Did words*
*fall from my tongue landing like poison?*
*Then I reflected to a deeper layer,*
*because maybe it wasn't me.*
*Maybe it was them.*
*A theory to soothe the bruises on my heart.*

# Other Worlds

*Wealth comes in many shapes...*
*Hardbacks and paperbacks*
*sit on shelves,*
*waiting patiently*
*for their pages to be turned.*
*But some rest with delight*
*knowing their stories*
*and poetic thoughts*
*have been liberated,*
*pages dog-eared for*
*another reading.*
*Seams of the bookcase*
*stretch like stitches*
*in too-tight jeans.*
*The bookcase itself*
*bulges like a belly satisfied*
*from a hearty meal.*
*I feel the excitement*
*of a child wandering*
*through a toy store*
*when I peruse new books*
*for the shelves...*
*Quiet moments await*
*for me to immerse*
*into those other worlds.*

# A New Sofa

*A simple wish,*

*a new sofa...*

*but now is not the time*
    *because our lab leans*

*against the sofa, chair, a leg*
    *with his soft fur*
        *bonding like bees to honey*

*so, I begin to rearrange*
    *with several ways*
        *to configure each piece*

*and who doesn't love options,*
    *like multiple-choice questions*
        *on a complex test?*

*I slowly spin, viewing the room after the labor is complete,*

    *and everything looks brand new...*

        *Who knew a simple wish could enlighten perspective?*

# Observations

*two hands on the wheel*
*orange poppies adorn the lane*
*dancing in warm breeze*

*rain downpours outside*
*dog snores from comfy round bed*
*paws overlapping*

*gray skitters along*
*the fence with perfect balance*
*gymnast with long tail*

*raindrops touch sidewalk*
*spring day in month of April*
*sunshine peeks through clouds*

*crow sits on rooftop*
*eyes observe all surroundings*
*wings flap for new meal*

*foghorn sings beneath*
*stars dangling in darkened sky*
*holding hands on pier*

# When life throws curveballs

**Emotions**
*Raw, hurtful*
*Aching, reeling, falling*
*Catches you by surprise*
*Reactions*

**Pain**
*Throbs, shocks*
*Stabbing, stinging, smarting*
*Halts activities like lightning*
*Agony*

**Perceptions**
*False, clouded*
*Mystifying, troubling, startling*
*Causes heartbeat to slow*
*Impressions*

# We find an escape

**Books**

*Stories, poetry*
*Compelling, transporting, entertaining*
*Turning pages is exciting*
*Paperbacks*

**Music**

*Songs, instruments*
*Playing, listening, singing*
*Dancing the night away*
*Melody*

**And a more personal reflection...**

**Music**

*Choir, piano*
*Harmonizing, recording, performing*
*Reveling in the spotlight*
*Dreams*

# A Two-Wheel Getaway

*Beautiful bikes admired*
*aesthetic differs*
*but enthusiast's passion runs parallel*
*Like-minded people walk*
*the lavish, green grounds*

*breeze swirls around faces*
*sunshine drops in now*
*and then, but scarves stay swathed, blowing in the wind*
*bikes glisten for adults*
*mini styles for youth*

*engines roar in distance*
*friendships established*
*though strangers when doors open, stories disclosed*
*history respected*
*a valued event*

# Fulfillment

*Joy could encompass*
*if you unfetter your goals*
*and dreams, functioning*
*parallel with purposes*
*to be recognized upon*

*the path that guides you*
*because they desire to shift*
*and slide however*
*their moods or penchants persuade,*
*longing to find fulfillment.*

# Ever So Gently

*Sometimes we get lost
in our thoughts...
losing focus of the stars
lighting up the night sky.
We tumble too deeply
into the frontal lobe,
allowing negative thoughts
to awaken, to throw a tantrum.*

*Remember, the breeze carries
burdens down rivers
and across oceans,
majestic trees sway with joy,
sheltering from shadows,
and the light shines even if only
a slight glimmer slips through.*

*Its glow will grow ever so gently
into a bright beacon of hope
rising with the golden sun
bringing clarity to our vision.*

*Ever So Gently*

# *Acknowledgements*

Many people helped in making this book a reality...

To my husband, Matt, who has been by my side for almost thirty-five years, thank you for getting that backpack on my back and for being the best partner in life.

To my daughter, Stephanie, thank you for those long, wonderful chats, and for always offering your support when it comes to my writing.

To my son, Michael, who painted the beautiful and gentle cover that I requested, and for helping me with the tedious formatting process.

Thank you to my sisters, Susie and Debbie, who continue to cheer me on in my writing endeavors.

This book would not have come to fruition without the many coffee meetings with my editor, Sharon Bluhm. Thank you so much, Sharon, for finding those tiny errors that could only be seen by a fresh pair of eyes. I enjoyed our chats and laughter, and I'm grateful for your candor and terrific suggestions.

I offer a big 'Thank you' to D. Wallace Peach for her marvelous endorsement, and for taking the time to read the entire manuscript to write a lovely, early review.

It has been an incredible journey to be a part of such a warm, blogging community. A huge thanks to my friends on WordPress for your perpetual support and encouragement.

I am beyond grateful to you all for supporting me to the finish line. xo

# *About the Author*

Lauren Scott is a poet, fiction writer, and memoirist, and has shared her writing on baydreamerwrites.com for over ten years. She has authored two collections of poetry: *New Day, New Dreams* and *Finding a Balance*. Her memoir, *More than Coffee*, was published in 2021, and she is a contributing author to the anthology: *Poetry Treasures 2: Relationships* released in 2022. Her work has been published on Spillwords Press where she was Author of the Month for May 2023.

As a teenager, Lauren and her best friend would lay on their stomachs on the floor and write in their journals. Their feelings about the boy crushes they had turned into rhyming poems, not devoid of giggles. From those early years, a bond between pen and thoughts formed. A new poem or story can develop from any aspect in life, so writing every day is as essential as brushing her teeth.

She lives in Northern California with her husband, Matt, of thirty-four years and their lab, Copper; they have two grown children. Her writing inspiration comes from her love of family, spending time in nature, and finding joy in the small things. Humor always finds its way into her life because without it, life would be colorless.

**To contact Lauren and read more of her work, visit her at the following:**

**Blog**: baydreamerwrites.com
**Shop**: https://www.amazon.com/stores/author/B08NCRH4MK
**Instagram**: @baydreamerwrites
**Facebook**: https://www.facebook.com/BaydreamerWrites
**Email:** baydreamer25@gmail.com

# *Other books by Lauren Scott*

*New Day, New Dreams (2013)* is a collection of poems that takes the reader on a romantic ride of happiness, heartbreak, and passion, along with exploring struggles in life, while being inspired to move forward. Adding humor and laughter to the mix is a delightful reprieve from heartbreak and hurt. This collection of poetry is a beautiful reminder of long lasting love, new beginnings, and showing appreciation of the special people in our lives.

*Finding a Balance (2015)* is Lauren's second book of poetry. This compilation speaks often of her emotions and spirit after finding out about a life threatening disease two years ago in a family member.

Many questions remain unanswered. In contrast to this sadness, Lauren has always possessed a romantic soul and is blessed to have celebrated twenty-six years of marriage to her husband and best friend. So from living in the darkness to finding the light again through faith and romance, she finds strength to move forward. This book takes the reader on a roller coaster ride of different emotions evoked from life and love, but regardless of what is thrown in her path, hope will always prevail.

*More than Coffee (2021)* is a memoir written in verse and prose. From the early woes of childhood and teen years, this compilation paints a picture of young dreams and fears. But as adulthood sets in, these dreams and fears change. *More than Coffee* touches on love and loss, nature and endurance, marriage and parenting. In these memories, humor diffuses fear and taking risks proves to be a powerful method in boosting self-confidence. Through it all, whether in the wilderness near a sparkling lake or in the comfort of home, there's nothing like a good cup of coffee. A poignant and reflective collection of short stories and poems that is best enjoyed sipping your favorite coffee roast.

www.ingramcontent.com/pod-product-compliance
Lightning Source LLC
Chambersburg PA
CBHW071329130726
47996CB00002B/682